Play It Again, Sam

ALLAN FELIX (Woody Allen) and his mentor, BOGART (Jerry Lacy).

PLAY IT AGAIN, SAM

Woody Allen

RANDOM HOUSE NEW YORK

PLAY IT AGAIN, SAM *was first presented on February 12, 1969, by David Merrick in association with Jack Rollins and Charles Joffe at the Broadhurst Theatre in New York City, with the following cast:*

(In order of appearance)

ALLAN FELIX	Woody Allen
NANCY	Sheila Sullivan
BOGART	Jerry Lacy
DICK CHRISTIE	Anthony Roberts
LINDA CHRISTIE	Diane Keaton
DREAM SHARON	Barbara Brownell
SHARON LAKE	Diana Walker
GINA	Jean Fowler
VANESSA	Cynthia Dalbey
GO-GO GIRL	Lee Anne Fahey
INTELLECTUAL GIRL	Barbara Press
BARBARA	Barbara Brownell

Directed by Joseph Hardy
Setting by William Ritman
Lighting by Martin Aronstein
Costumes by Ann Roth
Associate Producer Samuel Liff

SYNOPSIS OF SCENES

The entire action of the play takes place in the apartment of Allan Felix on West 10th Street in New York.

ACT ONE

Scene 1: A late summer afternoon
Scene 2: Later that night

ACT TWO

Two weeks later

ACT THREE

The following morning

Act One

The house lights dim and we hear the voices of Humphrey Bogart and Mary Astor in a scene from "The Maltese Falcon." Presently the curtain rises on ALLAN FELIX *watching the movie on his TV set in the living room of his apartment on 10th Street, between Fifth and Sixth avenues, in New York City.*

The living room is one of three rooms, the other two being a small but adequate bedroom and small but adequate kitchen, both of which are offstage in opposite directions. Up left there is a door which is the entrance to the apartment and which opens right in on a railed platform which serves as an office area; there are two sets of steps leading down to the living room, and between them, under the railing, a padded bench.

The living room itself is a reasonably spacious room, typical of the type found in old Village brownstones: cheery, with good-sized windows that overlook a tree-lined block from the second floor. It has a wood-burning fireplace and is furnished with a youthful warmth that includes books and records, a large photo of Bogart, comfortable chairs and an inviting sofa. It is an apartment that rents for about a hundred and sixty-five dollars a month and has been furnished and lived in for the past two years by the Felixes, a young married couple.

3

ALLAN FELIX *is a slight, bespectacled young man of about twenty-eight or twenty-nine who looks as if he just stepped out of a Jules Feiffer cartoon. He earns a decent living as a writer of articles and reviews, some literary but mostly cinematic, as he is a film buff, for a little intellectual film magazine. He daydreams of someday doing something important in either literature or film.*

ALLAN *daydreams a lot, in fact, his mind is a hyperactive mass of preposterously neurotic contradictions that make the world a little too much for him. He is nervous, shy, insecure, and has been in and out of psychotherapy for years.*

At the rise of the curtain ALLAN *is alone in a swivel chair watching "The Maltese Falcon." The film is in the final sequence wherein Bogey tells a surprised Mary Astor that he is going to turn her in despite the fact that he loves her. The soundtrack precedes the curtain for a line or two . . . He watches a bit after the curtain is up, sighs, crosses to the set and turns it off.*

ALLAN   How does he do it? What's the secret? It's the movies that's the secret. Maybe if I took two more aspirin I'd feel better. That's two—four—six aspirin. (*He picks up an empty aspirin bottle on the coffee table*) I'm turning into an aspirin junkie. Next thing you know I'll be boiling the cotton at the top of the bottle to get the extra. What's the matter with me—why can't I relax? I never should have signed those papers. (*He sits on the swivel-chair hassock*) Let her take me to court. Two years of marriage down the drain . . . like that . . . I couldn't believe it when she told me two weeks ago. She was like a stranger, not like my wife, like a total stranger.

(*Dream light rises in the office area.* NANCY *appears in a wrapper, drying her hair with a towel, and crosses to the end of the railing on the platform*)

NANCY   I don't want any alimony. You can have everything. I just want out.

ALLAN   Can't we discuss it?

NANCY   We've discussed it fifty times. It's no use.

ALLAN   Why?

NANCY   I don't know. I can't stand the marriage. I don't find you fun. I feel you suffocate me. I don't feel any rapport with you, and I don't dig you physically. For God's sake, don't take it personal!

(*She exits; the light fades*)

ALLAN   (*Rises and paces left and right*)   Oh, I won't take it personal. I'll just kill myself, that's all. If only I knew where my damn analyst was vacationing. Where do they go every August? They leave the city. Every summer New York is full of people who are crazy till Labor Day. And so what? What if I reach him? No matter what I say, he tells me it's a sexual problem. Isn't that silly? How can there be a sexual problem? We weren't even having relations. Well, once in a while. But she used to watch television during it . . . and change channels with the remote-control switch. (*He sits in the swivel hassock*) What's the matter with me? Why can't I be cool? What's the secret?

(*Dream light rises.* BOGART *appears in a trench coat*)

BOGART   There's no secret, kid. Dames are simple. I never met one who didn't understand a slap in the mouth or a slug from a forty-five.

ALLAN   I could never hit Nancy. It's not that type of relationship.

BOGART   Relationship? Where'd you learn that word? From one of those Park Avenue headshrinkers?

ALLAN   I'm not like you. At the end of "Casablanca," when you lost Ingrid Bergman, weren't you crushed?

BOGART (*Crosses up the left steps*)   Nothing that a little bourbon and soda wouldn't fix.

ALLAN   See, I don't drink. My body will not tolerate alcohol.

BOGART   Take my advice and forget this fancy relationship stuff. The world is full of dames. All you got to do is whistle.

(BOGART *exits and the dream light fades*)

ALLAN (*Pacing*) He's right. You give 'em an inch and they step all over you. Why can't I develop that attitude? Nothing a little bourbon and soda couldn't heal. I have one thimble full of bourbon, I run out and get tattooed. On the other hand, why should a divorce bother me so? What the hell—maybe I'm better off without her. Why not? I'm young . . . I'm healthy . . . I got a good job . . . this could be an opportunity to step out a little . . . if she can swing, so can I. I'll get broads up here like you wouldn't believe. I'll turn this place into a night club. Swingers, freaks, nymphomaniacs . . . salesgirls from Paraphernalia . . . She didn't want me—I'm not going to push myself on her. (*He sits in the swivel chair*) I couldn't believe the things she said to me the day she left.

(*Dream light rises in the office area.* NANCY *enters with bag, gloves and scarf*)

NANCY   I want a new life. I want to go discothequing and skiing and to the beach. I want to drive through Europe on a motorcycle. All we ever do is see movies.

ALLAN   I write for a film magazine, they send me. Besides, I happen to like movies.

NANCY   You like movies because you're one of life's great watchers. I'm not like that. I'm a doer. I want to participate. I want to laugh. We never laugh together.

ALLAN   How can you say that? I don't know about you, but I'm constantly laughing—I chuckle, I giggle, I guffaw occasionally. Besides, why didn't any of this come up while we were dating?

NANCY   Things were different—you were more aggressive.

ALLAN   Everybody is during courtship. It's only natural. You try and impress the other person. You can't expect me to keep up that level of charm. I'd have a heart attack.

NANCY   Good-by, Allan. My lawyer will call your lawyer.

ALLAN   I don't have a lawyer . . . have him call my doctor. (NANCY *exits and the dream light fades.* ALLAN *paces*) She thinks she's some hot stuff. She's no swinger. She's a product of the City College cafeteria. Next thing you know she'll be smoking pot—she'll think it's hip. I smoked pot once. Had a bad reaction . . . tried to take my pants off over my head. It's 'cause I'm guilty. I'm always so guilty over everything. She leaves me and I'm worried how she'll make out. (*The door buzzer sounds*) There's Dick and Linda. Thank God for Dick. He's my best friend, but I must not use him as a crutch. (*There is another buzz*) I'll use him as a crutch.

(*He opens the door.* DICK, *a nice-looking young executive type, and his lovely wife* LINDA *enter*)

DICK (*Moving along the railing*)   Allan, are you all right?

8

LINDA (*Closes the door and crosses to the end of the railing*) Oh, you poor thing.

DICK Why didn't you call us as soon as she left?

ALLAN I didn't want to bother you.

DICK Not bother us! For God's sake, what are friends for?

LINDA What reason did she give for wanting a divorce?

ALLAN (*He moves to the swivel chair, then sits on the corner bench*) She wants to laugh. She doesn't laugh enough. Insufficient laughter, that's grounds for divorce. And skiing—she wants to go skiing. She wants to ski down a mountain laughing like an idiot.

DICK Just let me call my office and let them know where I am. I rushed right out of a business meeting the minute you called. They must've thought I was crazy.

LINDA (*She places her purse on the bench*) Have you heard from her?

ALLAN I heard from the firm of Schulman and Weiss; they had me sign some papers, and Nancy went to Mexico. It's funny. We went to Mexico on our honeymoon. Spent the entire two weeks in bed. I had dysentery.

9

(*During the above and the following speeches,* LINDA *puts books from the floor by the coffee table on a shelf above the bar; she puts magazines from the sofa corner on a table behind the sofa; she gets a mug from the bar, a sweater from the end of the sofa, TV trays and the aspirin bottle from the coffee table, and in general cleans up the place*)

DICK (*Into the phone*)   Hello, George? Did they agree to the terms? Oh hell. Well, if we blow it, we blow it.

LINDA   Don't you cook anything but TV dinners?

ALLAN   Who cooks 'em? I suck 'em frozen.

DICK   Let me tell you where you can reach me. I'll be at Gramercy 7-9205 for a while, then I'll be at Murray Hill 5-4774 for fifteen minutes, then I'll be at Templeton 8-5548, then I'll be home, that's LE 5-8343. Right, George.

LINDA   There's a phone booth on the corner—you want me to run down and get the number—you'll be passing it.

(*She exits into the kitchen*)

DICK   I'm sorry, Allan.

ALLAN   She wants to be a swinger. All of a sudden married life is no good.

DICK   Don't get all worked up.

(LINDA *enters from the kitchen with paper toweling,
which she puts on the desk, and continues to tidy
up the apartment as the two men talk. She dusts
around the office area, then puts the papers from
the floor around the wastebasket into the wastebasket, and the wastebasket under the desk.*)

ALLAN   I gave her a home with affection and security.
This was a little girl I found waiting on tables at the
Hip Bagel. I used to come in every night and overtip
her. A dollar fifty on a thirty-five-cent check!

(LINDA *takes the robe off the railing, and the towel
and T-shirt off the desk chair*)

DICK   Nancy was impulsive. We all knew that about her.

ALLAN   She didn't leave impulsively. She talked about it
for months. I just couldn't believe she'd go through with
it. I'm such a naïve jerk. I'm lying in bed with her and
she's looking up lawyers in the yellow pages.

DICK   It's good you found out now. You're young. You
can make new lives.

(LINDA *takes the things into the bedroom*)

ALLAN   Young? I'm twenty-nine. The height of my sexual
potency was ten years ago.

DICK Look at the bright side. You're free. You'll go out. You'll meet exciting new girls, you'll flirt, there'll be parties, you'll have affairs with married women, sexual relations with girls of every race, creed and color.

(LINDA *comes out of the bedroom, moves down toward the steps, picks up a plastic pillow and puts it on the bench*)

ALLAN Ah, you get tired of that. Besides, those things never happen to me. I managed to fool one girl into loving me and now she's gone.

DICK See how he downgrades himself? Don't you think there are plenty of women in the world who would find him attractive?

LINDA Huh? . . . Oh, er . . . of course.

DICK (*Sits on the sofa*) The world is full of eligible women.

ALLAN Not like Nancy. She was a lovely thing. I used to lie in bed at night and watch her sleep. Once in a while she'd wake up and see me. She'd let out a scream.

LINDA He really loved her. I feel like crying.

DICK Why do you feel like crying? A man makes an investment—it doesn't pay off.

LINDA Could I get an aspirin? I'm getting a little headache.

DICK He's having a breakdown and you're getting sick.

LINDA Don't get upset.

DICK I'm not getting upset. I had a very rough day today.

ALLAN *You* want an aspirin?

DICK No.

ALLAN I ate all the aspirins. What about Darvon?

LINDA That's okay. My analyst once suggested Darvon when I had migraines.

ALLAN I used to get migraines, but my analyst cured me. Now I get tremendous cold sores.

LINDA I still do. Big ugly ones—from tension.

ALLAN I don't think analysis can help me. I may need a lobotomy.

LINDA With mine on vacation, I feel paralyzed.

DICK The two of you should get married and move into a hospital.

ALLAN You want a Fresca with your Darvon?

LINDA Unless you have apple juice.

ALLAN Oh, apple juice and Darvon are fantastic together.

LINDA Have you ever had Librium and tomato juice?

ALLAN I haven't personally, but another neurotic tells me they're unbelievable.

DICK Could I get a Coke with nothing in it?

(ALLAN *exits to the bedroom;* LINDA *puts the papers in the hall*)

LINDA He's suffering for her so. It's kind of sweet in a way. Would you suffer for me like that?

DICK Sure I'd suffer, but I wouldn't go crazy. You're like him. The two of you can get emotionally wrapped up in a weather report.

LINDA He never should have married Nancy.

DICK He never mentioned anything. I thought they were getting along.

LINDA That's because you're so busy all the time. You never see what's going on around you. Didn't you think it was strange he was married and yet he still couldn't get a date for New Year's Eve?

DICK   Why are you getting so overwrought?

LINDA   These things upset me. I'm experiencing a wave of insecurity.

DICK   You're experiencing a wave of insecurity? May I tell you what happened to me today? I bought one hundred acres of land in Florida this morning. It turns out ninety-eight of them have quicksand. My syndicate wanted to build a golf course. Now what? The only thing we can do is build a three-hole golf course with the biggest sand trap in the world. Why did this have to come up when I'm on the verge of a million things?

LINDA   You're always on the verge of a million things.

DICK   I can't help it. That's what I do, Linda. I look for openings, I keep on my toes, I play the market, I make brilliant deals like this quicksand thing.

LINDA   Dick, you're doing brilliantly. You're only twenty-nine years old and you've already filed for bankruptcy twice.

DICK   Oh come on, darling, don't get upset. Could I be any more crazy about you? Jesus, I tell him to take it easy . . . If I was in his shoes I'd go nuts. Now come on, we've got to get him over this.

LINDA   If I knew a nice girl for him.

DICK   You know models. There must be somebody in your agency.

LINDA   Not that many single ones.

DICK   What about Carol?

LINDA   Engaged.

DICK   And Doreen?

LINDA   She's living with a priest.

DICK (*He has a brainstorm*)   What about Zorita? That model at Don's party?

LINDA   For Allan? My God, she'd eat him alive. There'd be nothing left but his glasses. No, this is going to be a little problem.

(ALLAN *enters with the pills and drinks*)

ALLAN   Y'know, I'm glad you two came over. I'm feeling a little better.

DICK   Listen, Allan, Linda and I are going out for dinner tonight. We'll invite some nice girl, and the four of us will go together.

ALLAN   Oh no, I don't think so.

DICK   Come on, you've got to get out of the house.

ALLAN   I haven't looked at another woman in two years. I'm out of practice. When I was in practice I was out of practice.

DICK   Come on, Allan. You've invested your emotions in a losing stock, it was wiped out, dropped off the board. What do you do? You reinvest . . . maybe in a more stable stock . . . something with long-term growth possibilities.

ALLAN   Who are you going to fix me up with—Merrill, Lynch, Pierce, Fenner, and Smith?

DICK   Come on, Allan, shape up.

ALLAN   A pretty girl? Because she'd have to be damn good to do anything for my morale at all.

DICK   Who can we get for him?

ALLAN   You mean you don't even have anybody in mind?

DICK   We've got several people in mind.

LINDA   What kind do you like?

DICK   He likes neurotics.

ALLAN   I like blondes. Little blondes with long hair and short skirts with big chests and boots and bright and witty, and perceptive.

DICK   Don't set yourself ridiculous standards.

LINDA   She must be beautiful? With long hair and a big bust?

ALLAN   Oh—and a good behind. Something I can sink my teeth into.

DICK   He was always very fussy.

ALLAN   That's right, but look at the result.

DICK   That's right, you never went out.

LINDA   Sally Keller is blonde and has a good-sized chest.

ALLAN   What's good-sized?

LINDA (*Makes a gesture with her hands*)   I don't know— like this.

DICK   She's not the brightest girl in the world.

ALLAN   What does she do?

LINDA   She dances in a cage at a discotheque.

18

ALLAN   Forget it.

DICK   Come on, you might even be able to get her into bed.

ALLAN   Into bed! With my luck, I wouldn't be able to get her into a chair.

LINDA   Well, the girls that look the way you want them to, don't usually have great minds.

DICK   I don't know why we're making such a fuss over a little pleasant dinner companionship.

ALLAN   I don't even want that. I'm still too attached to Nancy.

DICK   Allan, forget Nancy. She's gone.

ALLAN   That's true. She wanted to be free to swing.

DICK   Come on, honey, think of someone.

ALLAN   I can just picture what she's been up to.

NANCY (*Enters*)   Oh Jeffrey, take me in your arms, hold me. To think that we two could meet here in a little town like Juarez, you divorcing Celia, me getting rid of what's-his-name. It's such a pleasure to be made love to by a tall, strong, handsome, blonde, blue-eyed man.

(*She exits*)

ALLAN   We're divorced two weeks, she's dating a Nazi.

LINDA   Hey, what about Sharon?

DICK (*It strikes him*)   What about Sharon?

ALLAN   I like the name.

LINDA   Sharon Lake. She works for Jack Edelman, the photographer. She's his assistant.

DICK   She's a bright girl and very cute.

ALLAN   Okay. Let's go.

DICK (*To* LINDA)   Call her.

LINDA (*Goes to the phone*)   Perfect.

ALLAN (*Beginning to falter*)   What are you going to tell her?

LINDA (*Dials*)   I'm going to see if she's free for dinner.

ALLAN (*Getting panicky*)   Don't tell her anything about the divorce. Maybe you better tell her my wife's dead.

DICK   Leave it to us.

ALLAN   I don't know if we should go through with this. (*Begins pacing*) The old tension is setting in. My stomach is jumping.

LINDA   (*Into the phone*)   Sharon Lake please. Linda Christie.

ALLAN   (*Puts his hands up to his ears, blocking out the sound, and prowls nervously*)   I don't want to hear this. *La-ummmmmmm-de-ummmmmmmmmmm* . . .

LINDA   Sharon? Hi. Linda. How are you? Good. Listen—

ALLAN   *Ummmm-ummmmmmm* . . .

LINDA   Dick and I are having dinner with a friend tonight and we thought you might want to join us.

ALLAN   *Ummmm-ummmmmmm* . . .

LINDA   No, that's nothing. We have the radio on. (*She beckons to* DICK *to help. He silences* ALLAN) Allan Felix. You don't know him. He's a friend of Dick's.

ALLAN   (*Prompting*)   Attractive. A writer. A widow—widower—my wife died in a mine-shaft explosion . . .

LINDA   He's a lot of fun. I think you'll like him.

ALLAN   Listen, if she doesn't want to—forget it. I don't need this aggravation.

LINDA   Okay. We'll pick you up with the car. Eight o'clock. A simple dress, oh sure . . . flats are okay.

ALLAN   Let her wear heels, what am I—Toulouse-Lautrec?

LINDA   Okay . . . We'll pick you up. Okay. Bye. (*She hangs up*) You're set.

ALLAN   (*He can hardly suppress his excitement*)   I have very mixed feelings. What if I have this chick in bed and Nancy comes in. Hoo-hoo.

DICK   Let's not hope for too much this first night, Allan.

ALLAN   (*To* LINDA)   Did she say anything about me?

LINDA   She doesn't know you. How could she say anything?

ALLAN   You know, you never said I was a widower.

LINDA   (*As she takes the Coke and Fresca into the kitchen*) I got you the date. You tell her the part about your wife's death.

ALLAN   Ooh, I'm excited.

DICK   (*Dials the phone*)   We'll pick Sharon up because she lives two blocks from us and then the three of us will pick you up. See you about ten after eight. I can't stay out late though, I have a business meeting tomorrow morning.

(LINDA *comes out of the kitchen with the four clean glasses and takes them to the bar*)

LINDA   Listen, if there's anything at all you want—if the dishes pile up or if you need a bed made . . .

DICK (*Into the phone*)   Hello, this is Mr. Christie. I'm leaving the Gramercy number now and proceeding due north to the Murray Hill number.

ALLAN   Let's eat at Tavern on the Green. It's a perfect night to dine out in Central Park.

LINDA   Wonderful, it's so romantic there.

DICK   I hate the food there. Besides I think it's going to rain. (*To* ALLAN) You be all right?

(DICK *and* LINDA *stop at the door*)

ALLAN   Sure—I'll be fine—I'll shower and douse my body with Canoe . . . Now I'm kind of looking forward to it. I'm excited.

DICK   Good-by.

ALLAN   I'm better . . . (*Closes the door; the expression on his face becomes serious*) I'm scared.

Blackout

SCENE 2

It is nearly eight that night. ALLAN *emerges from the bedroom, tie around his neck, and goes to the mirror over the bar. He is a mixture of anticipatory excitement, guilt and nerves as he tries to get his hair to fall satisfactorily.*

ALLAN   I cannot get my damn hair to stay down . . . this hot weather is murder on it. I'm not a bad-looking guy . . . chin's a little weak . . . what the hell . . . she shouldn't be disappointed. What does she expect? Rock Hudson? I'm a normal decent-looking guy . . . maybe slightly below normal. I wish she'd seen me before . . . I hate to be there on a blind date when the girl sets eyes on me. What if she looks at me and laughs or screams? Will you relax! Has a girl ever once reacted by laughing or screaming? Once. That little coed from Brooklyn College came to the door, saw me and passed out . . . but she was weak from dieting. What the hell . . . Bogart was short . . . didn't bother anybody.

BOGART   (*Appearing at the archway*)   You're starting off on the wrong foot, kid.

ALLAN   Negative, you mean?

BOGART   Sure. You're letting her get the best of you before the game starts. What's that stuff you were putting on your face?

ALLAN   Canoe. It's an after-shave lotion.

BOGART   And the other stuff?

ALLAN   That was Mennen spray deodorant, Lavoris, and Johnson and Johnson baby powder.

BOGART   For Christ's sake, you're going to smell like a French cathouse.

ALLAN   I need them.

BOGART   Why? You ashamed to sweat?

ALLAN   I want to make an impression.

BOGART   Y'know, kid, somewhere in life you got turned around. It's her job to smell nice for you. And whatever you do, don't tell her you don't drink. She'll think you're a Boy Scout. And don't get nervous—the only bad break you could get is if she turns out to be a virgin or a cop.

(He exits)

ALLAN   With my luck she'll turn out to be both. He's right. A lot of girls get turned on by a masculine, earthy quality. I shouldn't have put so much Binaca under my arms. I want to create a good subliminal impression without being too pushy. Hey, I better memorize some photography terms, if she's a photographer's assistant. (*He crosses to the magazine rack and pulls out a magazine, crossing back to the coffee table as he reads*) " 'Not only is there a great qualitative difference between my Nikon and my other cameras,' says ace photographer Greg Barnett, 'but my Nikon is built sturdy enough to withstand the throwing around I give it when the outdoor shooting gets rough.' " (*Drops the magazine on the coffee table*) I'm going to charm this girl. Wouldn't it be great if Sharon and I hit it off at first sight? Sure, why not? They say dames are simple. I never met one who didn't respond to a slap in the mouth or a slug from a forty-five. C'mere, Sharon.

> (DREAM SHARON *appears from the slot, slightly disheveled; she is wearing no shoes or stockings. "As Time Goes By" plays softly on the piano*)

DREAM SHARON   Oh Allan, you are fantastic . . . up until tonight, the doctors had said that I was frigid. I want to thank you for proving them wrong.

ALLAN   If you've got any friends with the same problem, bring them around.

DREAM SHARON   When Dick and Linda spoke of you, they used terms like genius and brilliant. They never said you were also an animal.

ALLAN   I'm sorry I had to slap you around, sweetheart, but you got hysterical when I said "No more."

DREAM SHARON   Oh Allan . . . Allan.

(*The lights change, the music fades and the buzzer sounds simultaneously.* DREAM SHARON *disappears*)

ALLAN   Yes?

LINDA (*Offstage*)   It's Linda.

ALLAN   Linda?

LINDA   I'm alone. (ALLAN *opens the door.* LINDA *enters with a jar of cocktail nuts in a bag*) Sharon's with Dick. They're parking. He sent me ahead just to make sure everything's okay.

ALLAN   Everything's fine . . . I didn't realize it was so late.

LINDA (*Takes two bowls out of the cabinet and puts nuts into each*)   Hey! What did you do? Break a bottle of shaving lotion?

ALLAN   You're kidding! I'm wearing too much?

LINDA   It's a touch strong . . . not terrible. Once we get into the air, you won't even notice it.

ALLAN (*Closes the bedroom door*) I just want to set up the place quickly.

LINDA (*Places a nut bowl on the coffee table*) The place is fine. We're only going to have a quick drink and go.

ALLAN (*Taking a book from the desk shelf and moving it to the downstage bench*) A few carefully placed objects will create the proper impression.

LINDA (*She puts the second bowl of nuts on the hassock*) You're not going to leave half-open books around like you're reading them?

ALLAN Why not? It creates a certain image.

LINDA You don't need an image . . .

ALLAN (*Takes a medal from the bar drawer*) I've got just the thing . . . my hundred-yard-dash medal.

LINDA You're joking! You're not going to leave out a track medal?

ALLAN (*Puts the medal on the swivel hassock*) Why not? I paid twenty dollars for it!

LINDA Just be yourself. She'll like you.

ALLAN (*Takes a Bartok record from the shelf above the desk*) I've got a big decision to make. Do I go with

Thelonius Monk or Bartok's String Quartet Number Five?

LINDA   Why don't you put on Thelonius Monk and leave Bartok carelessly strewn about?

ALLAN   (*Puts the Bartok record against the rail on the bench*)   Brilliant! That's exactly what I'll do.

LINDA   (*Gets bottles out of the bar and puts them on top*) I've never seen anyone go through so much trouble to impress a date. Particularly such a casual date. If you devoted this much interest and care with Nancy, I don't see why she left you.

ALLAN   (*Finding a Monk record on the shelf*)   Oh, I did. I used to write her poems. And take her to little candle-light restaurants and order in French and then the waiter would bring all the wrong things.

LINDA   (*At the corner of the bench*)   Maybe if you had leaned across the candlelight and kissed her . . .

ALLAN   I tried, and she'd say, "Christ, not here, people are staring." Then once at a great little bistro on Second Avenue, my sleeve caught fire. (*Puts the Monk record on the phonograph and plays it. LINDA laughs*) So you laugh at it, it's funny, right? She took it as a symbol of my clumsiness, which I guess it was. (*The door buzzer sounds. ALLAN snaps to attention*) Finesse . . . tremendous poise . . . I'm an absolute master.

29

LINDA Right. I'll get the ice.

(*She exits to the kitchen as* ALLAN *answers the door.* DICK *enters with* SHARON LAKE, *a very nice girl, attractive, but not the sex machine of* ALLAN'*s vision. However,* ALLAN *is sufficiently impressed to be rendered speechless*)

DICK Allan, this is Sharon.

SHARON Hello.

ALLAN Ah . . . er . . .

(*He stands dumbfounded, his hand on the door.* DICK *directs* SHARON *to the living room, thumps on the door to release* ALLAN's *hold and closes the door*)

SHARON (*Sitting on the left end of the sofa*) I was just telling Dick, I have some friends on this block. In the house across the street. Do you know the Gibsons?

ALLAN . . . the Gibsons? . . . No . . .
        (DICK *gives* ALLAN *a push into the room*)

SHARON Hal and Eleanor Gibson. They're a great couple. He's an interior decorator.

ALLAN (*At the sofa*) Oh really? That's sort of a hobby of mine.

SHARON (*Looking around, not overly impressed*) Oh . . . uh-huh . . .

ALLAN The key to decorating is to avoid looking like you used a decorator.

DICK (*At the railing*) I've got to make one fast call.

LINDA (*Entering from the kitchen with a water pitcher and ice bucket; she goes to the bar*) Hi!

SHARON Hi! . . . Linda?

LINDA Yes?

SHARON Are you wearing Jasmine?

LINDA Me? No . . . (LINDA *and* ALLAN *realize simultaneously that the pervading scent is from* ALLAN) What are we drinking?

DICK J and B on the rocks.

SHARON I'll just have a little Harvey's Bristol Cream, please.

ALLAN The usual. (LINDA *looks at him quizzically*) Bourbon and water.

(LINDA *goes to the bar and pours the drinks*)

SHARON Oh . . . a bourbon man.

ALLAN   Yeah, I gotta cut down on it. I'm putting away a
quart a day.

(*He sits on the sofa*)

DICK (*Into the phone*)   Hello, this is Mr. Christie. I'm no
longer at Lehigh 5-8343. I'll be at . . . What? Did he
leave a message?

(DICK *sits at the desk to take a few notes*)

LINDA (*Delivering a glass of sherry to* SHARON *and moving
back to the bar*)   Sharon did a movie.

ALLAN   Oh?

SHARON   Underground.

ALLAN   A stag film?

SHARON   Underground. You know—very arty sixteen-mil-
limeter.

LINDA (*Taking a drink to* DICK *at the desk and going
back to the bar*)   Allan's interested in cinema.

SHARON   What do you do?

ALLAN   I'm a writer. Nothing major. For *Film Quarterly,*
You know—essays, criticism . . . reviews . . .

SHARON This film I made got very good reviews. And I got singled out. Of course, I was the only girl in it with nine men.

ALLAN Oh really? What was the film called, maybe I saw it?

SHARON "Gang Bang." They have the raunchiest titles, but it wasn't a bit sexy . . .

DICK (*Finished at the desk, he crosses to join* SHARON *and* ALLAN) This is ridiculous. I have to get a phone for my car, Volkswagen or not.

ALLAN Volkswagen!

(*The music starts to build*)

LINDA (*Delivering a glass to* ALLAN) You were all out of bourbon, so I made it straight water. (*She joins the group, sitting on the hassock with her own drink*) It's so humid. I think it's going to rain.

SHARON Maybe that's why I have this headache; I get sinus attacks.

ALLAN Really? You should have them drained.

(*The music builds*)

DICK (*Sits in the swivel chair*) That's why it's silly to go to Tavern on the Green.

33

SHARON   Do you think you could turn the music down a bit?

(ALLAN *crosses to the office area*)

DICK   What's the point of going to an outdoor restaurant if it's going to rain?

LINDA   You used to like to take me walking in the rain.

ALLAN   I love the rain . . . it washes memories off the sidewalk of life . . .

> (*As this purple prose hangs in the air,* ALLAN *turns to the phonograph, where he accidentally knocks the tone arm, causing an ear-splitting scratch. All cringe.* DICK *spins around in the swivel chair*)

LINDA   Gee . . . you really have a delicate touch.

DICK   (*Rising and crossing to the hassock; he takes a nut*) Allan's a little tense. He's had a little misfortune with his wife . . .

SHARON   His WIFE?

> (ALLAN *takes the Monk jacket and replaces the record, keeping the record jacket in his hands*)

LINDA   Dick . . .

DICK   Ex-wife . . . she's gone . . .

ALLAN She's dead.

SHARON How awful!

LINDA Well no, she's not dead.

ALLAN Technically not dead . . . but we're not dating.

DICK She left him.

SHARON I'm sorry.

DICK (*Crossing to the phone*) Why don't I call and make a reservation at the Hong Fat Noodle Company in Chinatown.

LINDA (*Joining* DICK) Here, I have the phone number in my purse.

ALLAN (*Joining* SHARON *on the sofa, the record jacket still in his hand*) I don't know if you like Thelonius Monk or not, but to me he has a wry, mirthful quality that's not at all accommodating to the casual listener, although his harmonic conceptions are often haunting.

SHARON You sound like the back of a record jacket. (ALLAN *tosses the album in back of the sofa*) Er . . . have you known Dick and Linda long?

ALLAN I've known Dick for years. I don't know Linda nearly as well. Dick's a great guy. A little overambitious maybe, but he's always been that way. He's like a kid brother to me. I'm always helping him out of one jam or another. He kind of looks up to me.

(ALLAN *crosses his legs, hooking his toe under the coffee table and tipping it, scattering nuts and debris.* DICK *and* LINDA *rush to set things right.* ALLAN *backs off in dismay*)

DICK (*Turning to* ALLAN) We're all set at the Hong Fat Noodle Company.

ALLAN Just let me get my sport jacket.

(*He limps off to the bedroom*)

SHARON . . . Is he on anything?

LINDA Um . . . oh . . . no.

DICK I'm just going to call my service and tell them where I'll be.

LINDA (*Clearing up the mess*) I hope you like Chinese food.

SHARON Oh sure . . . Linda, I've just got to make it an early evening . . . I've got a terrible day tomorrow.

LINDA Oh, I'm sorry.

DICK (*Into the phone*) Hello. This is Mr. Christie. If Mr. Milton from the Chase Manhattan Bank calls, I'll be at the Hong Fat Noodle Company in Chinatown. That's Canal 8-6321.

(LINDA *hands* SHARON *the photography magazine from the floor.* LINDA *puts her and* SHARON's *glasses on the bar.* DICK *crosses to* LINDA *and gives her his glass*)

SHARON Hey! Look at this! Greg Barnett. You remember Greg? . . . Jack's old partner . . . (*She reads*) " 'There is a great qualitative difference between my Nikon and my other cameras,' says ace photographer Greg Barnett, 'but my Nikon is built sturdy enough to withstand the throwing around I give it when the outdoor shooting gets rough.' " I wonder how much they paid him to say that?

ALLAN (*Enters from the bedroom and crosses to* SHARON) I'm ready! And you've gotta let me order because I'm an expert on Chinese food.

SHARON Good! I'm starved . . . we had such a rough day today trying to photograph little children.

ALLAN (*Giving his arm as they start out*) Oh really? Photography is a hobby of mine. In fact, I've been having a little trouble with my cameras lately. See, I feel there is a great qualitative difference between my Nikon and my other cameras, but my Nikon is built sturdy enough to withstand the throwing around I give it when . . .

Curtain

Act Two

The curtain rises on ALLAN. *It is two weeks later, and he has had a pretty discouraging time of it. He is at the sofa, with the phone on the coffee table, as he thumbs through an old address book.*

ALLAN   Mildred Denberg . . . can't even remember her. Marion Drayson . . . she sat behind me in Civics. Toby Kovack . . . yeah . . . I remember her! She was a pushover, with those great legs and those freaky parties. *(He dials)* Hello? Is this the Kovack residence? Ah . . . how can I get in touch with Toby? Oh she is? I see. No, thanks, let it go, forget it. *(Hangs up)* The wife of Rabbi Kaplan! I'm cursed. I cannot get a break. *(Thumbs through the book)* Marilyn Perry. The queen of Dubrow's. *(Dials)* Hello, is this the Perry residence? Ah, is Marilyn there? *(Rises and crosses)* You know where I can reach her? An old friend from Midwood High School—Allan Felix. I dated her once. Do you remember? I'm stunned! It was eleven years ago . . . that's right . . . short, with red hair, and glasses—no, that's cleared up. How can I get in touch with her? Oh really? She still feels that way? You know, it's been eleven years now. When did you speak to her? Last week . . . and she specified she didn't want you to give me the number? Well, good-by, Mrs. Perry. No, that's all right. (*Hangs up and puts the phone on the bench*) I don't know how much longer I can take this. I miss being married. These past two weeks have been terrible. At least Linda's been fixing me up with some of her friends. But with every girl something goes wrong. First there was that photographer's assistant, Sharon. I made a mess of that. Then the next night there was Gina.

(GINA *enters as the lights change and* ALLAN *falls into step with her as they cross to the downstage railing*)

GINA Good night, Allan. (*He moves to embrace her*) Don't!

ALLAN Why not?

GINA I'm Catholic.

ALLAN I'll convert.

GINA Besides I didn't take my pill today.

(*She exits through the bedroom door, slamming it behind her*)

ALLAN That's all right . . . I took an extra one! (*The lights are restored*) What'd I do wrong? She treated me cold from the second I showed up at her door with a Whitman Sampler. And what about Vanessa? That was only a week ago . . . you'd think by then my luck would have begun to change.

(*The lights dim to a late-night romantic mood.* VANESSA, *exotically dressed, appears and glides to the sofa, where she reclines. Soft music plays in the background.* ALLAN *joins her*)

VANESSA I've had many men . . . my first at twelve. After that it was an endless stream. Poets, writers. I lived in a house with five actors. Some were gay, but what does it matter? I straightened them out. It was a challenge. My life was a continual round of orgies. I took on the entire Tau Epsilon Phi Fraternity at Yale in three hours. It's still a record in New Haven. I've always thought of sex as something wonderful and open . . . to be enjoyed as fully and frequently as possible. (ALLAN, *increasingly aroused, finally can restrain himself no longer and lunges for her. She screams and jumps up*) Aaaaagh! What do you take me for?

(*She exits as the lights are restored*)

ALLAN How did I misread those signs? . . . What am I going to do? I've practically used up every friend Linda has. I may have to resort to desperate measures to meet women . . . like going up to East Hampton or hanging around Bloomingdale's stocking counter. Ah . . . I'm too shy to do those things alone. Linda would come with me even if Dick's busy. Dick and Linda sure have been great. I've dragged them everywhere to help me find girls. Linda seems to like it. I know she enjoyed that evening at the discotheque.

> (*He sits on a corner of the bench. The lights dim.* DICK *and* LINDA *join* ALLAN *and sit at the corner of the bench. On the platform behind them a fantastic little blonde in a glittering dress is bumping and jerking to drive you crazy. The music blares*)

LINDA   Gee, this is fun. We haven't been to a discotheque in such a long time.

ALLAN   I'm getting a heart attack. I can't believe that girl.

DICK (*Into the phone*)   I'm at Lehigh 4-3605.

ALLAN   She's a doll! I would sell my mother to the Arabs for that girl!

LINDA   Well, ask her to dance. You've been staring at her for an hour.

ALLAN   I can't . . . I don't know her.

DICK (*Puts the phone down, and turns to them*)   Come on. I can't stay any longer. I have to get up early tomorrow and sue some friends.

LINDA   You want to dance one dance, honey?

DICK   We can't do those dances. They're undignified.

You've got to be under sixteen to look good. But you two can stay, just don't get home too late. Good luck.

(DICK *exits through the kitchen*)

ALLAN   I love you, Miss—whoever you are—I want to have your child.

(*The music segues to a relatively slow number*)

LINDA   Get up and do it.

ALLAN   I can't dance—have you ever seen my body move? It's like a printing press.

LINDA (*Dragging him to the platform*)   Come on . . .

ALLAN   I'm scared—please—no—no . . .

LINDA   Start dancing . . . that's it . . . keep count . . . one . . . two . . . one . . . two. Now talk to her. Go ahead.

ALLAN   One . . . two . . . one . . . two . . .

LINDA   Try something more meaningful.

ALLAN   Three . . . four . . . three . . . four . . .

LINDA   No! . . . Go on . . .

45

ALLAN Er . . . good evening, Miss. Would you be interested in dancing?

GO-GO GIRL Sure!

> (*The music switches abruptly to a wild rock rhythm as the* GO-GO GIRL *thrashes appropriately. In a desperate effort to look good* ALLAN *attempts a few vaguely Spanish fandangos.* LINDA *has slipped offstage at the start of this. The* GO-GO GIRL *dances her way toward the center of the stage, sees* ALLAN *and erupts into derisive laughter, backing off. The lights restore and the music fades*)

ALLAN What I need is a more intellectual girl . . . that's where my appeal is . . . that's why last Monday afternoon the Museum of Modern Art seemed such a good idea . . .

> (*The lights fade, leaving an aisle of light across the forestage.* LINDA *enters wearing a raincoat.* ALLAN *joins her*)

LINDA Um . . . look at that Salvador Dali . . . if you could have any painting in the world, what would you pick?

> (*Through these speeches they drift toward the left of the stage*)

ALLAN A Van Gogh. Any Van Gogh.

Diane Keaton, Woody Allen and Anthony Roberts as LINDA CHRISTIE, ALLAN FELIX and DICK CHRISTIE, with Lee Anne Fahey, the GO-GO GIRL, in the background.

LINDA Me too. I feel some kind of mystical attraction for Van Gogh. Why is that?

ALLAN All I know is that he's a great, great painter and he cut his ear off for a girl he loved.

LINDA That's the kind of thing you'd do for a girl.

ALLAN Yeah . . . (*Embarrassed*) I'd really have to like her a lot.

LINDA I wonder if Dick would cut his ear off for me.

ALLAN I don't think you better ask him. He's been very busy lately.

LINDA It must be fantastic to be loved so intensely.

ALLAN I guess we may as well split and see if there's any action at the Guggenheim.

> (*A pretty blonde, the* INTELLECTUAL GIRL, *wearing low-cut jeans and a shirt tied high, exposing a lovely midriff, wearing moccasins and a shoulder bag, enters*)

LINDA Here comes one.

ALLAN Ah . . . she is one.

LINDA Go ahead . . . speak to her.

ALLAN I'll get arrested.

LINDA Go ahead before the room gets crowded and you feel ashamed.

ALLAN (*To the* INTELLECTUAL GIRL) Uh . . . that's quite a lovely Franz Kline, isn't it?

GIRL Yes, it is.

ALLAN What does it say to you?

(LINDA *sits in the swivel chair and turns upstage*)

GIRL It restates the negativeness of the universe. The hideous, lonely emptiness of existence—nothingness—the predicament of man, forced to live in a barren, Godless eternity, like a tiny flame flickering in an immense void—with nothing but waste, horror and degradation—forming a useless, bleak straitjacket in a black, absurd cosmos.

ALLAN What are you doing Saturday night?

GIRL (*Exiting*) Committing suicide.

ALLAN What about Friday night? Intellectual women are a pain in the neck—got to be the right mixture of brains and passion. Now Linda's got it all. She's so easy to be with . . . like that day last week in Central Park . . . she was sweet, and friendly, and tried her best to be helpful.

(ALLAN *moves to the hassock, sits and starts to mime rowing a boat. Appropriate sounds are heard.* LINDA *has been sitting in the swivel chair and spins around to face front*)

LINDA   Don't you understand, Allan? You have a lot going for you. You're bright and funny and even romantic, if you could only believe it. You put on a false mask as soon as you meet a girl.

ALLAN   It's different around you. You're my friend's wife. I'm not trying to impress you.

LINDA   I keep telling you . . . be yourself. The girl will fall in love with you.

ALLAN   Listen, you've been so nice this past week, spending your time with me.

(ALLAN *stops rowing and pulls a small tissue-wrapped object from his pocket*)

LINDA   I'll tell you the truth, I'm having a ball.

ALLAN (*Takes the present from his pocket*)   I wanted to get you this because it's your birthday.

LINDA   How did you know it was my birthday?

ALLAN   You mentioned it one day and I remembered it because it's the same date my mother had her hysterectomy.

LINDA (*Moving to kneel on the hassock just behind him*) It's lovely—it's beautiful—a tiny plastic skunk.

ALLAN   It looked so cute in F. A. O. Schwartz and I heard you say skunks are your favorite animals . . . it doesn't function . . . it just exists . . .

LINDA   I'm so touched. I don't know what to say.

(LINDA *sits back in the swivel chair, swings around to face upstage and exits.* ALLAN *goes back to rowing; then, as the lights change, he finds himself back in his living room*)

ALLAN   Linda's a great girl. I think Dick kind of neglects her. Hell, I told him so the other night. If I'm his friend, I've got to speak candidly to him. He's gotta learn to take it easy and treat her a little better.

(*The lights change and* DICK *enters*)

DICK (*Crosses to the sofa, puts his briefcase on the coffee table*)   How could you get her a birthday present and I forget? Why didn't you warn me?

ALLAN   She's your wife. I assumed you knew.

DICK (*Crosses to the phone on the bench*)   I'm up to my ears in work. I purchased fifty lots for building in Tennessee, it turns out they're radioactive. I'm taking a beating.

(*He dials*)

ALLAN   Maybe if you just took Linda out once in a while.

DICK   That's the farthest thing from my mind. Besides, I went to a discotheque with both of you last week.

ALLAN   That was one night, two weeks ago, and you left early, and you wouldn't dance with her, and you forgot her birthday.

DICK   I didn't forget completely. I was late. My secretary picked her up some jewelry.

ALLAN   Your secretary? That's not very personal. Women like personal junk . . .

DICK   You know what it is to be stuck with fifty lots that are radioactive? What am I going to build, an X-ray center? (*Into the phone*) Hello, Miss Carson? What are the figures on the new contract, fifteen hundred or eighteen hundred? . . . Thank you.

(*He hangs up and crosses back to the sofa*)

ALLAN   So once in a while you take her dancing or on a picnic.

DICK   Maybe, who knows . . . maybe I got married too young. She was so beautiful . . . first in her class at Bard College. I'll never forget that prom weekend, there was moonlight, and soft music, I looked at her with her hair spilling down her shoulders and thought—she's the perfect corporate image for a young executive.

ALLAN I hate to tell you, pal, but that sounds a little callous.

DICK Oh come on, Allan, she knows I love her. Christ, I'm crazy about her, and have been since the second I met her. Meanwhile, between my quicksand and my radioactivity, I'll be driving a cab soon.

(*The lights change and* DICK *vanishes*)

ALLAN Some guys don't know a good thing when they have one. (*He rises from the hassock and crosses to the desk*) Well, I gotta stop daydreaming . . . I'm going to lose my job if I don't finish my essay on Anna May Wong. (*The doorbell buzzes. He answers it and it is* LINDA) Hi.

LINDA Hi.

ALLAN What's the matter?

LINDA I hope I'm not bothering you . . . what do you have for an anxiety attack? I need a tranquilizer.

ALLAN I got everything. I'm a drugstore.

LINDA I have a throbbing in the pit of my stomach.

ALLAN How do you know it's anxiety? How do you know it's not fear?

LINDA My stomach feels jumpy.

ALLAN   You find it hard to breathe?

LINDA   A little—I feel frightened, and I don't know over what.

ALLAN   I get that.

LINDA   Is it fear or anxiety?

ALLAN   Homosexual panic.

(*He exits to the bedroom*)

LINDA   Oh . . . I always get this way when Dick goes on a business trip.

ALLAN (*Offstage*)   Oh?

LINDA   He had to fly to Cleveland for the day. I got up, helped him pack, drove him to the airport, and threw up in the United Airlines terminal.

ALLAN (*Returning with a pill and a glass of water*)   That's a good terminal. I've thrown up there.

LINDA   I don't know what it is that upsets me so.

ALLAN   Fear of separation. It's an interesting psychological phenomenon. I had to go to Washington once when I was married, and even though I was the one leaving, I got sick. Yet when I returned, my wife threw up.

53

(*He returns the glass to the bedroom*)

LINDA My analyst would say I'm feeling guilty because I really want him to go.

ALLAN (*Reenters from the bedroom*) Come on . . . I don't understand you . . . you got everything going for you. You're bright . . . people photograph you for magazines, so you know you're beautiful. You read, you play Bach on the recorder, you're happily married. I mean, why should you be a mass of symptoms?

LINDA Well, you've got a lot going for you, and you're a mass of symptoms. I guess it happens to us when we're children . . . you know, you think you're ugly and your parents get divorced . . . you feel abandoned . . . you must have had the same thing.

ALLAN My parents didn't get divorced . . . although I begged them to.

LINDA (*Sits on the sofa*) Do you really think I've got a lot going for me?

ALLAN I do. And I'm fussy. I don't know how I can afford to be, but I am.

LINDA It's funny. I never thought you liked me very much. You know, when I married Dick.

ALLAN I thought you didn't like me so much. I thought maybe you thought I was an oddball.

LINDA I never really knew you. I mean, we never spent
any time together. Dick described you as the first guy
who sat through "The Maltese Falcon" twelve times in
two weeks. Then when the four of us went out together
you acted differently than now. I feel I've really gotten
to know you in the past few weeks and I've come to a
very interesting conclusion. You definitely are an oddball
. . . but you're one of the best people I've ever known.

ALLAN That's nice. Because you're the only really platonic
friend I've ever had.

LINDA I like a platonic relationship. They're so much less
complicated. Not that I'm down on male-female rela-
tionships—although marriage is a tough proposition at
best.

ALLAN It's disastrous.

LINDA I know. Dick and I are constantly, quote, reapprais-
ing our marriage.

ALLAN Are you?

LINDA Sure. Especially in the last year. You know, he's
gotten deeper and deeper into his work and my interests
have gone in another area. That is, they always were.
There are certain things we both need that we don't
give each other.

ALLAN Marriage can be a very lonely thing. But not so
lonely as I've been since I've been single.

55

LINDA Hey, no date tonight?

ALLAN Ah . . . I had a date but she called it off . . . some kind of Polish holiday.

LINDA Well, why don't we go out to dinner and maybe a movie?

ALLAN I got a better idea. Why don't we have dinner here and see what's on the "Late Show"?

LINDA You have anything here for me to cook?

ALLAN I have some frozen steaks and a bottle of champagne.

LINDA What are you doing with champagne? You going to launch a ship?

ALLAN I tried cooking here last week—to impress a date. I tried to make beef stroganoff in the pressure cooker.

LINDA How'd it taste?

ALLAN I don't know. It's still on the wall.

LINDA Is the grocery on the corner still open?

ALLAN Yes.

LINDA (*Rises and takes her purse from the coffee table*) I'll be right back. I'll get us some asparagus and salad and dessert. I love to cook and I never get the chance—Dick's so busy all the time.

ALLAN   And get some candles. I love to eat by candle-light.

LINDA   I'll cook and you open the champagne. But not if I'm going to be the only one who drinks it.

ALLAN   I'll drink one or two with you, but you've got to promise to put me to bed if I try and dance naked. (LINDA *exits*) Hey, this'll be fun! I have a terrific rapport with Linda. I hate to see her depressed. It'll be cozy. (*Puts pillows from the couch by the fireplace*) Spending an evening in . . . nice summer rain outside . . . (*Closes the shutters*) It's just damp enough to have a small fire. Adjust the lighting in here. (*Turns on a light on the bar*) Create a little atmosphere. (*Picks up the address book from the coffee table, puts it on the desk shelf, starts for the kitchen*) Get out the champagne. Women are suckers for champagne . . . it makes them crazy. (*Out from the kitchen*) Wait a minute . . . what the hell am I doing! Women are suckers for champagne. This is Linda. Dick's wife. Linda. Remember? Gee, I got carried away for a minute. What the hell was I thinking?

(LINDA *enters. Soft music plays in the background. They meet on the sofa*)

LINDA   Dinner was wonderful, Allan. The steaks were superb, the champagne perfect. I'm so glad we decided

57

to stay home and spend a quiet evening together. You're the only man I've ever met who really holds my interest.

ALLAN You should feel flattered. Not many women are deep enough to know what it is I'm all about.

LINDA (*Kissing him*) I'm sorry for acting like a schoolgirl —I couldn't help myself. I've wanted to do that for so long now.

ALLAN We mustn't. It's forbidden.

LINDA But these things happen. Nobody plans them.

ALLAN Yes, but you're not free.

LINDA In my heart I'm free. I can't repress it any longer. At first I thought you were just a helpless, mixed-up child, but I didn't really know you then. Now I believe you're everything I ever dreamed of loving.

ALLAN You poor thing. How you must've suffered— wanting me so.

LINDA My darling, I need you. I need to possess you body and soul.

ALLAN Which would you like to begin with?

LINDA (*Rises and crosses to the mantel*) We were meant for each other. If we miss this opportunity we'll regret it as long as we live.

ALLAN My head says it's insane, but my heart says, don't believe your head, it's a lying head. (LINDA *vanishes*) This is terrible. I'm sitting here making love to my best friend's pillow.

BOGART (*Enters*) So, you finally fell in love with her.

ALLAN I just got carried away for a minute.

BOGART Come on, kid, you don't have to feel guilty.

ALLAN Guilty over what? Two lonely people with a tremendous amount in common have dinner together. We're platonic friends.

BOGART There's nothing platonic about the way she feels about you.

ALLAN How can you tell?

BOGART What do you want her to do—attack you?

ALLAN She's my friend's wife.

NANCY (*Enters*) Of course she is. She'll tell Dick and he'll beat you to a pulp.

BOGART Look, she loves you, not him.

NANCY He's not the romantic type.

BOGART He could be if he tried.

NANCY Don't listen to him.

BOGART Don't listen to her.

ALLAN I'm getting a headache.

(NANCY *and* BOGART *exit*)

DICK (*Enters*) Allan, I want you to do me a favor.

ALLAN Yes?

DICK I've fallen in love with another woman. Don't ask me
how—it just happened. We're going off together to live
in Alaska. Oh, she's an Eskimo. I know that you and
Linda have always been fond of one another and I
thought perhaps after I'm gone you might look after her.
It would mean a lot to me.

ALLAN Of course.

DICK Well, I'm off to Alaska. If you need me I'll be at
Frozen Tundra 7-0659.

(*He vanishes*)

ALLAN She is always complimenting me. I know she likes
me. But does she like me that way? What the hell? I
could test her. I could maybe make an advance . . .
what could possibly go wrong?

(*The dream lights go on.* LINDA *appears and crosses
to the sofa. Music plays in the background*)

LINDA   Dinner was wonderful, Allan. The steaks were superb, the champagne perfect.

(*She sits on the sofa*)

ALLAN   (*Crosses to sit on the sofa*)   Linda, tonight the earth shook.

LINDA   What?

ALLAN   Linda darling . . .

LINDA   Don't . . .

ALLAN   It was meant to be . . .

LINDA   Allan, take your hands off me, you must be crazy.

ALLAN   Linda, my love . . .

LINDA   Allan, I'm a married woman. Rape!

ALLAN   Shhhh . . . you'll wake up the whole house!

LINDA   Think of Dick—he's your best friend.

(*They rise*)

ALLAN   My sleeve is caught on your zipper!

LINDA   Thank God, Dick gave me this tear-gas pen!

(*She mimes the pen business as a loud jet spray sound is heard;* LINDA *exits.* ALLAN *covers his face, coughing as the lights are restored*)

ALLAN (*Pacing*) Look, let's not get carried away. I'm not an appealing guy. The thought that a girl like Linda could go for me . . . I'm kidding myself. Where the hell is she? By now she could have had her steak and been home!

(*The doorbell buzzes.* ALLAN *opens the door.* LINDA *enters for real with a bag of groceries*)

LINDA I feel so light. That Librium is beginning to work.

ALLAN (*Takes the bag*) Maybe you better not have any champagne.

LINDA (*Takes the candles from the bag*) Oh no, what the hell—if I get too out of hand you can always call the police.

ALLAN (*Goes into the kitchen with the bag*) How long did you say Dick was out of town for?

LINDA He'll be back tomorrow.

ALLAN (*Enters from the kitchen*) There's a new Godard film at the Sutton . . . I thought maybe we could go—

LINDA (*Gets the candlesticks from a shelf above the bar*) Come on—you're kidding . . . we're all set for here

. . . Besides, it's starting to rain. Besides, I remembered that great Ida Lupino movie is on Channel Four . . . you know, where she's married and she suddenly becomes involved with her husband's best friend.

ALLAN   How does it end?

LINDA (*Sits on the sofa and puts the candles in the holders*) She kills them and herself.

ALLAN (*Crosses to the sofa*)   Let's go out.

LINDA (*Puts the candles on the mantel, turns on the sconce switch, then picks up some pillows near the fireplace*)   I want to see that Ida Lupino movie. It's a fascinating theme. You think it's possible to love two people at once?

ALLAN (*Moves to the center of the sofa*)   What do you mean?

LINDA (*Crosses to* ALLAN *at the sofa and puts one pillow on the sofa*)   A wife, happily married, suddenly finds she loves another man . . . not that she doesn't love her husband . . . just that . . . she loves someone else . . . you think it's very possible?

ALLAN   Do you?

LINDA   Very. Very possible and probably very common. Love is such a strange phenomenon . . . strange and exquisite . . .

BOGART (*Appears*) Go ahead. Make your move.

ALLAN Uh—

BOGART (*Crosses to* ALLAN *on the sofa*) Go ahead. Take her and kiss her.

ALLAN Uh—(*Paralyzed to act on this advice*) Uh—

LINDA Is something wrong?

BOGART Go ahead. She wants it.

ALLAN Wrong? No—I—

LINDA I better begin our food.

BOGART Go ahead. Kiss her.

LINDA Yes?

BOGART Hurry! Before she moves out of position.

ALLAN I—can't do it.

BOGART Kiss her, kid!

ALLAN I—I—can't!

LINDA I'll be right back.

> (*She turns and goes off to the kitchen, putting another pillow on the sofa*)

BOGART (*Sits in the swivel chair*)   Well, kid! You blew it.

ALLAN   I can't do it. She'll misunderstand it. I invite her over and I come on like a sex degenerate! How does it look? What am I, a rapist?

BOGART   You're getting carried away. You think too much. Just do it.

ALLAN   We're platonic friends. I can't spoil that by suddenly coming on. She'll slap my face.

BOGART   I've had my face slapped plenty of times.

ALLAN   Yeah, but your glasses don't go flying across the room.

BOGART (*Rises and crosses to the corner of the sofa*)   You're going to disappoint her.

(LINDA *enters with two glasses of champagne*)

LINDA   Here we are. Start on this. (*Hands him a glass and crosses below the coffee table to the other corner of the sofa*) Hey, did you read in the papers, another Queens woman was raped?

(ALLAN *practically spits up his first swallow*)

ALLAN   Oh really? I was nowhere near Queens. Do they know who did it?

65

LINDA (*Sits on the sofa*) No. They haven't a clue. He must be very clever.

ALLAN (*Sits on the opposite end of the sofa*) You've got to have something on the ball to rape so many women and get away with it. Ah-ha . . .

> (*He's trying to be light. He looks at* BOGART, *who doesn't smile*)

LINDA I think if anyone ever tried to rape me I'd pretend to go along with it and then right in the middle pick up the nearest heavy object and let him have it. (BOGART *and* ALLAN *look troubled*) Unless, of course, I was enjoying it.

> (*Both men brighten*)

ALLAN They say it's the secret desire of every woman.

LINDA Well, I guess it depends on who does the raping.

ALLAN Well look, why dwell on morbid things? Odds are you'll never get raped.

LINDA Not with my luck. (*Closes her eyes happily*) Um— I feel so light. The drink went right to my head. I'm floating.

ALLAN (*Agreeing*) Um.

BOGART Go ahead, kiss her.

ALLAN I can't.

BOGART She's ready.

ALLAN How do you know?

BOGART Believe me. I know.

ALLAN She'll pull back. I feel it.

BOGART She's sitting and waiting. Don't screw up.

ALLAN Okay—I'm going to try . . . But I'm gonna go slow . . . (*He begins inching into position. Very scared*) If she jumps I'll pretend it was a joke.

BOGART Hurry.

ALLAN She better laugh. (*Just as he's about to strike, the phone rings with shattering clarity and he jumps with a near heart attack*) Ohmigod! Didn't expect that! (*He goes to pick up the phone*) What a start . . . (*Into the phone*) Hello? Dick? Hi . . . What? Yes . . . she is. She dropped over—very unexpectedly. I had a Polish date. Two good friends—we're going to have one fast dinner, then right out . . . Huh? Yes, I'm all right. I'm fine. Say, aren't you in Cleveland? Oh, then this call is costing you money . . . I'll put her on . . . (*Offers her the phone*) He wants to speak to you. From Cleveland.

(BOGART *crosses above the sofa*)

67

LINDA (*To* ALLAN, *en route to the phone*) Are you upset over anything?

ALLAN Oh no . . . I was just startled . . . (LINDA *sits on the bench and speaks into the phone.* ALLAN *crosses to one end of the sofa*) This is ridiculous. I'm going to cause an international incident. I want her out. I can't handle this.

LINDA Hello, darling.

ALLAN Hello, darling. She loves him. What am I kidding myself?

BOGART (*Crosses to the sofa*) Will you relax? You're as nervous as Lizabeth Scott was before I blew her brains out. All you gotta do is make your move and you're home free.

ALLAN This is crazy. We'll all wind up on the front page of the *National Enquirer*.

LINDA Okay. Good-by. I will. (*She hangs up*) Dick sounded a little down. I think he's having some trouble in Cleveland.

ALLAN How come he never takes you with him when he goes on those out-of-town trips?

LINDA (*Crosses to the sofa*) I'm afraid to fly. My analyst thinks that's an excuse. He never asks me along, though.

Who knows? Maybe he's got something going on the side.

(*This last said jokingly*)

ALLAN (*Sits on the sofa, left of* LINDA) Would that bother you?

LINDA Sure. I mean, not if I didn't know.

ALLAN I know he'd be very hurt if you ever had a casual affair with somebody else.

LINDA I don't think I could have a casual affair.

ALLAN No?

LINDA I don't take those things lightly. If I fell for another man there'd have to be something more there than a little fling. I'd have to feel something more serious, in which case my marriage would be in question. Are you shaking?

ALLAN I'm chilly.

LINDA It's not very cold. I'm not the type, though. I don't think I could take the excitement involved. Anyway, I'm not glamorous enough.

ALLAN Oh, you are. You're uncommonly beautiful.

LINDA When I go to a discotheque and see all those

beautiful young girls I feel like life has passed me by. I should be selling chocolates at Fanny Farmer.

ALLAN You're crazy! Those girls are not in your league.

LINDA Keep talking. You're saving my life. I have such an inferiority complex.

BOGART Say, you're handling yourself very well. Now kiss her.

ALLAN Please—

BOGART You built up to it beautifully.

ALLAN I just don't have the nerve.

BOGART Tell her how beautiful she is again.

ALLAN I just told her!

BOGART Again.

ALLAN Y'know, you are really one of the most beautiful girls I've ever known.

LINDA I don't know what to say to that.

ALLAN I mean really beautiful—unbelievably beautiful— fantastically beautiful—

BOGART All right already.

LINDA   It's been so long since anybody said that to me.

BOGART   Now move closer to her.

ALLAN   How close?

BOGART   The length of your lips.

ALLAN   That's very close.

BOGART   Come on. Move.

(ALLAN *does*)

ALLAN   Now what?

BOGART   Tell her that she moves something in you that you can't control.

ALLAN   You're kidding.

BOGART   Go ahead.

ALLAN   From me it's corny.

BOGART   She'll love it.

ALLAN   It's like Fred Astaire looks great in tails, I look silly.

BOGART   Leave Fred Astaire out of this. Say something.

7 I

ALLAN   I love the time we've spent together.

LINDA   So have I.

ALLAN   Was that all right? I don't want to use your other line about moving something in me.

BOGART   You're doing fine, kid. Tell her she has the most irresistible eyes you've ever seen.

ALLAN   Eyes you—you eyes—you—you have the *most* eyes of anybody . . .

LINDA   Your hand is trembling.

ALLAN   It is?

BOGART   That's because you're near.

ALLAN   Pardon me?

BOGART   Tell her that!

ALLAN   That's because you're near.

LINDA   You always know what to say, don't you?

BOGART   Tell her you've met a lot of dames but she's really something special.

ALLAN   That she won't believe.

BOGART   No?

ALLAN   I've met a lot of dames but you are really something special.

LINDA   Really?

ALLAN   She bought it.

BOGART   Now put your right hand around her shoulder and draw her near.

ALLAN   I don't want to—I'm afraid.

BOGART   Go ahead. (ALLAN *does it*) Now get ready for the big move and do exactly as I tell you.

   (NANCY *enters with a gun*)

NANCY   I warned you to leave my ex-husband alone. (*She shoots* BOGART. NANCY *and* BOGART *exit*)

LINDA   Well, I guess I'll start the steaks.

ALLAN   Linda, your eyes are like two thick steaks.

   (*He has summoned his courage and tries to kiss her. She bangs backwards, knocking over the standing lamp on the sofa table*)

LINDA   Allan, don't! I'll pay for the lamp.

73

ALLAN   It's all right! I think I love you!

LINDA   I insist on paying for the lamp!

ALLAN   (*Still in a wrestle*)   Forget the lamp!

LINDA   I'm so clumsy—will you take ten dollars!

ALLAN   (*Still going for her bobbing head*)   Forget the damn lamp! Give me five bucks, we'll call it square!

LINDA   (*Disengaged, she rises and gets her purse from the bench*)   Allan—don't—

ALLAN   Don't get the wrong idea—it was a joke—I was testing you—you don't think—I meant a platonic kiss—not a whole kiss—here—

LINDA   I better go.

ALLAN   (*Following*)   Linda . . .

LINDA   I really better go.

ALLAN   Linda.

LINDA   Please. I'll be fine. (*Awkwardly, she goes*)

ALLAN   (*Alone, frantic*)   I attacked her! What did I do? I'm a vicious jungle beast! She's going to tell Dick! She's panicky now! By the time she gets home she'll be hysterical! She'll probably go right to police headquarters! What kind of idiot am I to try a fool thing like that! I'm not Bogart. I never will be Bogart. What'll I tell Dick? I'm a disgrace to my sex. I should work in an Arabian palace as a eunuch. (*The doorbell buzzes*) There's the Vice Squad.

(*He turns and opens the door.* LINDA *enters*)

LINDA   Did you say you loved me?

(*They kiss*)

ALLAN   Play it again, Sam!

(*The music becomes louder*)

Curtain

Act Three

The curtain rises on ALLAN *and* LINDA, *the following morning, after they have "done it." It has been a mixed thing for them—beautiful and traumatic. They are on the sofa with coffee mugs.*

ALLAN Two lonely people with a tremendous amount in common thrown together continually—before we know what's happening, we're in love . . . we fight it as long as possible, we're alone on a rainy summer evening, Dick's a thousand miles away, we couldn't fight it any longer, I took you in my arms and we made love. Then we each got upset stomachs. The main thing is that we're honest.

LINDA I still can't believe it.

ALLAN I haven't slept that well in years. Is it noon yet?

LINDA It's seven.

ALLAN Seven? I didn't realize it was so early. You were fantastic last night.

LINDA Thanks.

ALLAN How do you feel now?

LINDA   I think the Pepto-Bismol helped. What were you thinking of while we were doing it?

ALLAN   Willie Mays.

LINDA   You always think of baseball players when you're making love?

ALLAN   It keeps me going.

LINDA   I couldn't figure out why you kept yelling "slide."

ALLAN   I think it'd probably be best if you told Dick.

LINDA   Dick?

ALLAN   I guess it'll come as a surprise, but . . .

LINDA   Oh . . . it'll be a surprise all right . . .

ALLAN   Make sure you tell him on a day that Wall Street closes high.

LINDA   Gee . . . the whole thing is complicated.

ALLAN   Listen, it happened, it happened—can't help that. It happened. It's not my fault. It's not your fault. The point is—you felt like a woman, and I felt like a man, and that's what those kind of people do.

LINDA   I did feel like a woman. You were wonderful.

ALLAN   I have a fantastic craving for breakfast.

LINDA   I'll make some. What are you in the mood for?

ALLAN   Steak and eggs, pancakes, butter and syrup, biscuits, and a big pot of coffee.

LINDA   (*Rising*)   Well! In that case, I'd better go downstairs and pick up a few things.

ALLAN   Don't bother . . . we'll go out.

LINDA   (*Gets her purse from the bench*)   No . . . no . . . I'll go. I need a little fresh air.

ALLAN   Take my raincoat, there's money in the pocket.

LINDA   Wait'll my analyst comes back from his vacation and finds out about this. He'll become a chiropodist.

(*She exits*)

ALLAN   You killer! You were incredible in bed last night . . . like Toscanini. Nancy should have been there —she'd have seen a master in action . . .

NANCY   (*Appears in dream light*)   Oh Allan, word's out all over Europe that you're the best thing in bed the United States has to offer.

ALLAN   You could have had some of this and you threw it away.

NANCY   I made a mistake. I know that now. Can't we start over?

ALLAN   It's too late. Linda and I are in love. We're going away.

NANCY   I've been a fool. (*Organ music plays*) Good-by, Allan, I'm going to become a nun. If I can't have you, the next best thing is God.

(*She vanishes*)

ALLAN   She's got a point there. Gee, I can't believe it. This bright, beautiful woman is in love with me. Of course she's in love with me. Why shouldn't she be? I'm bright, amusing . . . sensitive face . . . fantastic body. Dick'll understand. Hell, we're two civilized guys. In the course of our social encounters a little romance has developed. It's a very natural thing to happen amongst sophisticated people.

DICK (*Appearing in dream light*)   You sent for me?

ALLAN   Yes.

DICK   Good.

ALLAN   Drink?

DICK   Quite.

ALLAN   Scotch?

DICK   Fine.

ALLAN   Neat?

DICK   Please.

ALLAN   Soda?

DICK   A dash.

ALLAN   Linda and I are in love.

DICK   It's just as well. I've come from my doctor. He gives
me two months to live.

ALLAN   Good, then you don't mind?

DICK   Not a bit.

ALLAN   Cheers.

DICK   Cheers.

(*He vanishes*)

ALLAN   (*Rises*)   Sure . . . things are going to be okay.
Hell, Dick and I have been through tougher situations
than this. Dick and I have been through a lot together.
He's my best friend. This is terrible. This is going to
hurt him . . . I know it.

DICK   (*Enters in dream light*)   Thanks a lot.

ALLAN   Dick . . .

DICK   (*Crosses left of the sofa*)   How could you? My wife
and my best friend. I trusted you both. I feel I've been

83

made such a fool of. I loved her. I loved you. Why didn't I see it coming? Me—who had the foresight to buy Polaroid at eight and a half!

(*He disappears*)

ALLAN   This is awful . . . he'll do something rash. Dick's an emotional guy. He'll kill himself. Kill himself? Did you ever think what he might do to you? Didn't you ever hear of the unwritten law? You take a guy's wife . . . you humiliate him. You've seen enough Italian movies. Dick's got a temper!

DICK (*Enters in undershirt and scarf*)   Bastado! Pezzo di curnutu. Tu mai tradutto me!

ALLAN (*Backing up the steps onto the platform*)   Ma non e vero.

DICK   Tu mi pigli per stupido!

ALLAN   Non e curpa mia.

DICK (*Leaps over the railing*)   Bugiardo! Proco! Carogna! Imbesile!

(*He draws a dagger*)

ALLAN   No . . . no . . .

DICK   Solo chisto me tuo sadisfari mio onore.

(*He stabs* ALLAN)

Diane Keaton, Woody Allen and Jerry Lacy as LINDA
CHRISTIE, ALLAN FELIX and BOGART.

ALLAN   Oh boy, that hurt! (DICK *exits.* ALLAN *stands at the railing*) This is ridiculous! What am I going to do? I love her. She loves me. We could have a wonderful life together. Why does Dick have to be in the picture? Hell, take it easy. Why do you have to make everything into a Warner Brothers production? She'll come back, we'll have breakfast together. Shape up. She'll be back in a minute. You'll spend the day together . . .

(*The doorbell rings.* ALLAN *opens the door to find* DICK *with his suitcase and coat*)

DICK   (*Leaves his coat and case at the railing*)   I had to come home, Allan. I have to speak to you. Allan, I think Linda's having an affair. I just called home. She's not there. These past few weeks she's seemed distracted, distant, little things only a husband would notice. You've seen her a lot these past couple of weeks . . . she's changed. The other night she talked about an affair in her sleep.

ALLAN   Did she mention any names?

DICK   Only yours. When I woke her and questioned her she said it was just a nightmare. (*He crosses up the steps and onto the platform*) I try to think of who it might be. It has to be someone I don't know . . . some guy she met through work . . . an agent, a photographer, some ad executive, or actor.

ALLAN   Why are you so upset . . . I thought she was just your corporate image?

DICK I love her. If she leaves me I'll kill myself.

ALLAN Since when are you so emotional?

DICK I've never been in love with anyone before. If I find out who the guy is I'll kill him, I swear. I've neglected her and now she's involved with some stud! (ALLAN *sits in the swivel hassock;* DICK *sits on the edge of the coffee table*) If I haven't already lost her to someone, I'm going to make up for everything to her. I'm going to change. I'm going to do everything I can to make her life with me exciting and fun because without her it wouldn't be worth living. I was up all last night in a Cleveland hotel room. I figured, all right, I'm losing her . . . too bad . . . I'll survive. Then I panicked and phoned her. She was out. When I called her here last night she said she was going home. Where'd she stay?

ALLAN (*Rising*) Calm yourself.

DICK (*Rises, crosses, then moves back to* ALLAN) I've got to find her. I've got to stop her and beg her forgiveness before it's too late. I want her to get on that plane with me and fly back to Cleveland. I want her with me all the time. I want to pamper her. I want to hear her laugh and speak . . . I'm sorry for carrying on like this Allan, but you're the only friend in the world who would understand.

ALLAN I . . . I understand.

DICK Look, if she calls, tell her I'll see her home. Tell her I've got to speak to her, will you?

86

ALLAN Sure . . . sure.

DICK Thanks . . . thanks a lot.

(*He gets his coat and suitcase and exits*)

ALLAN (*Sits on the coffee table*) I'm going to faint. How could I tell him? The guy's desperately in love with her. I never realized how much. He never realized how much. I couldn't do that to a stranger, much less a friend. But what if it's too late. What if Linda's really hooked on me now? You know, once a woman's been made love to by somebody who can really do it great! I was fantastic last night! I never once had to sit up and consult the manual. Love is very different for a woman. It's a complicated phenomenon. I don't know what to expect. I've never broken off with a woman before.

(*The dream lights go on.* LINDA *enters in a trench coat and goes up the steps to the railing end*)

LINDA So you think it's as simple as that?

ALLAN (*Goes up the platform to* LINDA) We have no choice.

LINDA You told me you loved me.

ALLAN Try to take it gracefully.

LINDA But the time we spent together, the closeness, the promises.

ALLAN Please, Linda . . .

LINDA You mean too much to me. I can't let you go.

ALLAN Linda, don't be difficult . . . I'm sorry.

LINDA Sorry's not enough . . . you think I'm a play toy.

ALLAN What can I say?

LINDA (*Bette Davis with a gun*) Give me the letter.

ALLAN What letter?

LINDA Philip, give me the letter.

(LINDA *backs* ALLAN *up through all this*)

ALLAN There is no letter.

LINDA I want the letter. Philip, give me the letter.

ALLAN Linda, you're going crazy.

LINDA You can't treat me that way.

ALLAN Don't pull the trigger—I'm a bleeder. (*The light fades and she vanishes.* ALLAN *crosses*) She'll kill me. Women are violence-prone. Bette Davis, Barbara Stanwyck . . . they're killers . . . I'll go away—I'll join the circus. I'll be a clown . . . I'll never take off my make-up . . . Like Jimmy Stewart.

(*The dream lights go on.* BOGART *appears*)

BOGART (*At the end of the railing*)   Pull yourself together, kid, you're hysterical.

ALLAN   I'm going to join the circus.

BOGART   You should feel encouraged. When you weren't coming on phony, you got a pretty good dame to fall for you. You never thought you could make it with dames. Well, you can.

ALLAN   But now it's got to end and I can't do it.

BOGART   It's not that hard, kid. Watch. (LINDA *enters. Music plays in the background*) C'mere, sweetheart.

LINDA (*Goes up the steps onto the platform with* BOGART) Yes, darling?

BOGART   It's over.

LINDA   What is?

BOGART   Us.

LINDA   Over?

BOGART   That's right, toots. Over. *Kaput.*

LINDA   That simple, eh?

BOGART   That's right.

LINDA   Supposing I say no?

BOGART Won't do you any good.

LINDA (*Pulls out a pistol and sticks it in his face*) And will this?

BOGART (*Takes the gun and slaps her in one cool move*) Come off it, Sugar. You never could use a rod.

LINDA (*Sobbing*) But why does it have to end before it can begin? Tell me why?

BOGART You play too rough for me, Sugar. It was you that killed Johnson. Parker found out about it so you killed him too. But that wasn't good enough for you. You wanted to finish me off. You knew you couldn't do it while I was facing you, so you figured you'd get me to turn my back. But not me, Sugar. Now come on. You're taking the fall. (LINDA *exits, sobbing*) That's all there is to it.

ALLAN For you, because you're Bogart.

BOGART Everybody is, kid. At certain times. You're doing something now I didn't think you had in you. You're passing up a real tomato because you don't want to hurt a guy. If I did that there wouldn't be a dry eye in the house.

ALLAN Yeah, but I'm broken-hearted over it.

BOGART That's all the more reason you can be proud of it.

ALLAN You think so?

BOGART   Sure. Listen, kid, there's other things in life besides dames and one of 'em is to know you did a right
thing for a pal. Think it over.

(*The doorbell buzzes.* ALLAN *goes to the door. It is*
LINDA. BOGART *moves down the steps*)

ALLAN   Er—grocery store not open yet?

LINDA.   No.

BOGART.   Tell her.

ALLAN   What?

BOGART   Tell her. Now.

(*He exits*)

ALLAN   Linda . . .

LINDA   Allan, do you realize what a wonderful thing has
happened?

ALLAN   Linda . . .

LINDA   Allan, the most beautiful thing in the world has
occurred right under our noses. We've had a wonderful
experience. Doesn't that surprise you? You didn't have
to do anything. Didn't have to leave any half-open books
lying around . . . you didn't have to put on the proper
mood music. I even saw you in your underwear with the
days of the week written on them.

ALLAN   Look, Linda, we've . . . got to call it quits.

LINDA Yes, I know. While I was out, suddenly everything became very clear, and when I asked myself do I really want to break up my marriage . . . the answer was no. I love Dick, and while someone as wonderful as you is very tempting . . . I can't think of my life without him.

ALLAN You can't?

LINDA He needs me, Allan . . . and in some unexplainable way . . . I need him.

ALLAN I know he needs you.

LINDA This is the first time I've ever been affected by anyone besides Dick—I'm already a little in love with you—and unless I stop it now I'll find myself too deeply involved to go back to him. I don't regret one second of what's happened because what it's done for me is to re-affirm my feelings for Dick.

ALLAN Go home, Linda . . . He's home waiting for you.

LINDA He is?

ALLAN He came by while you were out. He wants you to go back to Cleveland with him. He'll explain it. Meanwhile, we'll just be good friends . . . I think I'd like that.

LINDA You're sure? You're not saying that to make things easy?

ALLAN (*Piano music starts in the background*) I'm saying it because it's true. Inside of us we both know you belong with Dick. (*Music*) You're part of his work, the thing that keeps him going. If that plane leaves the ground and you're not with him, you'll regret it. Maybe not today, maybe not tomorrow, but soon and for the rest of your life.

LINDA That's beautiful.

ALLAN It's from "Casablanca." I waited my whole life just to say it.

LINDA (*Goes up the steps and kisses* ALLAN) Good-by.

(*She exits*)

NANCY (*Enters*) Poor Allan—I told you this would happen.

ALLAN (*Crosses to the sofa*) Are you kidding? She was in love with me—you heard her.

NANCY Meanwhile she's back with Dick.

ALLAN I gave him a pretty good run for his money . . . without even trying—that's the key.

BOGART (*Enters*) You tell her kid—it's all yours now.

ALLAN I'm going to do something I should have done a long time ago. I'm going to forget you.

NANCY What! Allan don't—no—don't—don't, nooo . . .

(*She gives a long wail as she backs out*)

BOGART Gee, kid, that was great. I'd have slapped her around a little myself, but you've got your own style.

ALLAN I do have a little style.

BOGART Well, kid, so long.

ALLAN You're leaving?

BOGART You don't need me any more. There's nothing I could show you, you don't already know.

ALLAN I guess that's right. The secret's not being you, it's being me. True, you're not too tall and kinda ugly. But I'm short enough and ugly enough to succeed by myself.

BOGART Here's looking at you, kid.

(*He exits. The doorbell buzzes. The piano music fades.* ALLAN *opens the door*)

BARBARA I'm sorry for bothering you. My name is Barbara Tyler. I just moved in upstairs and I'm all alone and I locked myself out. Could I use your phone?

ALLAN Sure, it's right over there.

BARBARA Thank you. (*Noticing* Film Quarterly *on the desk*) *Film Quarterly!* You're not *the* Allan Felix who writes for *Film Quarterly,* are you?

ALLAN Yes, I am.

BARBARA I just did my Ph.D. on cinema for the New School, and I used some of your articles for reference. They're very clever.

ALLAN (*Piano music starts*) Thank you.

BARBARA I particularly liked the article you wrote on "The African Queen."

ALLAN That was one of my favorite movies.

BARBARA It was quite a departure for Bogart.

ALLAN Well, you see, the thing about Bogart that most people don't know is that . . .

Curtain

ABOUT THE AUTHOR

WOODY ALLEN, one of today's leading comedians, was born in Brooklyn. While still in high school he wrote and sent jokes to newspaper columnists, and soon found himself giving material to Peter Lind Hayes and Herb Shriner on radio and television. He then added Sid Caesar, Art Carney, Kaye Ballard, Carol Channing, Garry Moore and Buddy Hackett to his stable of clients. Seven years ago Mr. Allen started to perform his own writing, which was autobiographical in nature. He was a success at New York's Blue Angel and St. Louis' Crystal Place, and then on television. His first film, *What's New, Pussycat?*, which he wrote and in which he starred, is one of the biggest successes in screen history. His play *Don't Drink the Water* was a Broadway hit from the time of its opening in 1966, and will be made into a film. Mr. Allen has also contributed to *The New Yorker* magazine and has made long-playing records.